Tarot: A Beginners Guide

By Gabby Benson

All rights reserved. No part of this publication may be reproduced or transmitted in any form or by any means, electronic or mechanical, including photocopy, recording, or any information storage and retrieval system, without permission in writing from the publisher

Contents

Introduction 7
CHAPTER 1 – The Cards 8
    Where to get the Cards and which to choose 8
        Looking After Your Cards 9
    The Tarot Deck 9
        The Minor Arcana 9
    The Major Arcana 14
    Interpreting the Cards 17
CHAPTER 2 – THE Major Arcana 20
    Other Links 20
    The Meaning of Cards 21
        The Fool 21
        The Magician 22
        The High Priestess 23
        The Empress 24
        The Emperor 25
        The Hierophant 26
        The lovers 27
        The Chariot 28
        Justice 29
        The Hermit 30
        The Wheel of Fortune 31
        Strength 32
        The Hanged Man 33
        Death 34
        Temperance 35
        The Devil 36
        The Tower 37
        The Star 38
        The Moon 39

- The Sun 40
- Judgement 41
- The World 42

CHAPTER 3 – The Suite of the Swords 44
- The Minor Arcana 44
- Brief, General Meanings 44
- The Meaning of the Cards 45
  - Kings of swords 45
  - The Queen of Swords 46
  - Knight of Swords 47
  - Page of Swords 48
  - Ace of Swords 49
  - Two of Swords 49
  - Three of Swords 49
  - Four of Swords 50
  - Five of Swords 50
  - Six of Swords 50
  - Seven of Swords 50
  - Eight of Swords 50
  - Nine of Swords 51
  - Ten of Swords 51

CHAPTER 4 – The Suit of Wands 52
- Brief, General Meanings 52
- The Meaning of the Cards 52
  - King of Wands 52
  - Queen of Wands 53
  - Knight of Wands 54
  - Page of Wands 55
  - Ace of Wands 56
  - Two of Wands 56
  - Three of Wands 56
  - Four of Wands 57
  - Five of Wands 57
  - Six of Wands 57

- Seven of Wands 57
- Eight of Wands 58
- Nine of Wands 58
- Ten of Wands 58

CHAPTER 5 – The Suit of Cups 60
- Brief General Meanings 60
- The Meanings of the Cards 60
  - King of Cups 60
  - Queen of Cups 61
  - Knight of Cups 62
  - Page of Cups 63
  - Ace of Cups 64
  - Two of Cups 64
  - Three of Cups 65
  - Four of Cups 65
  - Five of Cups 65
  - Six of Cups 65
  - Seven of Cups 66
  - Eight of Cups 66
  - Nine of Cups 66
  - Ten of Cups 66

CHAPTER 6 – The Suit of Pentacles 68
- Brief, General Meanings 68
- The Meanings of the Cards 68
  - King of Pentacles 68
  - Queen of Pentacles 69
  - Knight of Pentacles 69
  - Page of pentacles 71
  - Ace of Pentacles 72
  - Two of Pentacles 72
  - Three of Pentacles 72
  - Four of pentacles 73
  - Five of pentacles 73
  - Six of Pentacles 73

- Seven of Pentacles ... 73
- Eight of pentacles ... 74
- Nine of Pentacles ... 74
- Ten of Pentacles ... 74

CHAPTER 7 – Spreads ... 76
- Hints on Giving a Reading ... 76
- The Ten Card Spread ... 76
- The Seven Card Spread ... 77
- The Bohemian Spread ... 78
- The Pyramid ... 79
- The 12-Month Spread ... 79
- The 21-Card Spread ... 80
- The Five Card Spread ... 81
- A Sample Reading ... 81

Conclusions ... 83
- Other Links ... 83

Introduction

No one can say exactly when the tarot cards were first used but they are at least medieval, if not older. Most people accept that the cards were introduced by the Italians, but again this is open to conjecture.

Many people look to tarot cards for fortune-telling purposes (known as cartomancy), associating them with the gipsy travellers who were instrumental in increasing their circulation throughout Europe. However, there is so much more that can be learnt from tarot. Many people, scientists included, are now looking at the psychological advantage of using tarot as an aid to learning more about ourselves and others, looking towards the mystic symbolism on the cards rather than their predictive purposes.

Many people scoff at the idea of cards being able to be used in a predictive way, and others think of them as The Devil's Picture book, but it is possible to use the cards to help ourselves and others, and I hope here to be able to give sufficient information for everybody to be able to use them, not only for their own purposes, but with friends and famIly. It is important to understand that, whatever use you put the cards to, whether it be for serious intent or not, they are not a game. They can indeed be fun, but they should never be treated lightly.

Most people can learn to read the cards. This will come more easily to some than to others. Each chapter in this book concentrates on a different aspect of the cards, and in the final chapter, we will practise a little, with different types of spread. Tarot cards are the forerunners of modern playing cards, and I shall try to show the similarities with standard cards, as well as the differences, in addition to giving clear and precise information as to the meaning of each card.

At this point I should point out that many people have slightly differing interpretations of the cards, and many professional readers will have ways of expressing the meanings which may be different from those given here in some way. However, the information in this book should be sufficient to start you off on the road to understanding tarot, and may lead to your wishing to undertake further research into the cards and using them in your daily life.

Remember what the tarot is not; it is not some infallible oracle, it is a set of very old pictures set down on pieces of paper. What we make of it is up to us!

CHAPTER 1 – The Cards

There are many different theories about how the word tarot came about and what it really means, but like the history behind the cards, it is not easy to give a definite answer to the question. Egyptian scholars maintain that the word has Egyptian origins, whereas other people think it is a derivative of the word tarotee, which was the design used on the back of cards. It is also suggested that the word tarot comes from the game of tarocco played in Italy in medieval times. Nobody really knows the answer, and maybe this has added to the mystique of the tarot cards over the years.

The tarot pack, whatever its origins, is still as current in its role today as it ever was. Many people are helped through using the tarot, whether it be from answers given, or sometimes even from answers not given; it causes people to look more closely at themselves, their conscious and subconscious thoughts and desires, and find a solution from within.

Where to get the Cards and which to choose

The first thing you need to study tarot is obviously a set of cards. Cards are available from a wide variety of outlets. Most people will find them on sale in New Age shops and centres, but they are also available at fairs and other shops not necessarily associated with the esoteric or mystic.

There is a wide variety of cards now available. Many of them have similarities in design, many are based on designs reflecting the general name given to the cards, such as Celtic tarot, Egyptian tarot etc. The commonest packs are the Marseilles cards, the Etteilla cards, the Rider-Waite cards, the Aleister Crowley cards, Tarot Classic cards and III cards (which are used in this book). These are but a few of the sets of cards available, and choosing what cards you want to use is a personal decision. There are scores of cards around for the newcomer to look at, but my advice would be to choose a pack with clear, standard definitions, and move on to the other types of cards at a later stage when you have mastered the subject.

There are indeed some beautiful sets of cards on the market. Those interested in the Kabbala will find many cards which feature Hebrew ideology. Some sets of cards follow the ancient packs of which some examples still remain. I personally have four different sets: one which I use at personal sittings; one which I use for postal consultations; one which I use for lecture purposes (on account of the clarity of the cards and their images); and the one which I started off with. A set of cards can cost anything from $10 (£7) to over $30 (£20), and many come with a small booklet giving information on the illustrations on the cards and the card meanings. You can also get cards for beginners, where the meanings are printed on the cards.

Looking After Your Cards

Some people like to keep their cards in special containers and it is not uncommon for professional readers to keep their cards wrapped in silk and then put in boxes. This, they feel, keeps them special and many believe helps to preserve their vibrations. However, it may just be a case of preserving the mystique!

What you keep your cards in is your concern, but please keep them separate from other cards, or in a special place on their own, so they do not get lost, mislaid or used by others. I would personally be horrified to find anyone playing with or using my cards without my permission or my being there. I have built up a personal link with my cards, which is why I use different cards for different purposes.

The Tarot Deck

The tarot deck in its complete form comprises 78 cards. These are split into the major and minor arcana, sometimes also known as the greater and lesser arcana.

The Minor Arcana

The minor arcana comprises 56 cards, which are divided into four suits numbered from Ace (I) to 10, with a King, Queen, Knight and Page. You will note the extra card here when comparing the cards to the standard playing cards we now have. When the cards increased in popularity, the Cavalier (or Knight) and Page (or Knave) were amalgamated into the Jack, and we arrived at a standard pack of 52 cards, plus the Joker (which is the Fool from the major arcana). The minor arcana cards are basically concerned with jobs, status and everyday things.

The suit names of swords, wands, cups and pentacles are the forerunners of the suit names we have now, and can be broken down as follows (please note, the representation of class systems is a generalisation, and for guidance only):

Swords or epees correspond to spades
Represent executive classes

Wands, sceptres, rods, batons or clubs correspond to clubs
Represent lower income groups

Cups, chalices, goblets or coupes correspond to hearts
Represent clergy/religious groups

Pentacles, coins, money, circles, discs or deniers correspond to diamonds
Represent merchant/business classes

You will see that some of the words are not English. Many terms are French or Italian and these languages will appear on the cards of the major arcana and also sometimes on those of the minor arcana. Don't worry! - you will not have to learn the foreign language concerned - just remember the category.

The four elements identified by the ancient Greeks can be connected to the minor arcana suits. The suit of cups is connected with water, wands with fire, swords with air and pentacles with earth. This can be extended to see cups as being emotions, wands challenge, swords mental matters and pentacles possessions, and ties in with the representative class list.

The court cards within the minor arcana can also be categorised - Kings are associated with power, Queens with support and creativity, Knights with new projects and Pages with new information. Court cards can be further divided into personality types, zodiac signs and physical types. In general terms only: cups are fair, plump, emotional and creative people and correspond with the water signs of Cancer, Scorpio and Pisces; wands are brown- or red-haired, well-built people, who are energetic and restless, and correspond with the fire signs of Aries, Leo and Sagittarius; swords are either very dark or very fair, tall, slim people with an unemotional, logical nature, and correspond with the air signs of Gemini, Libra and Aquarius; and pentacles are short, dark people, who are earthy, practical and stubborn, and correspond to the earth signs of Taurus, Virgo and Capricorn.

The Major Arcana

In addition to the 56 minor arcana cards, there are 22 major arcana cards. These are sometimes also known as trump or triumph cards, and it is these cards which have the most elaborate designs and have led to the tarot's mystical reputation. These cards are usually numbered, with the exception of the Fool card, which has no number, and is the equivalent of the Joker in a pack of standard cards. However, unlike the Joker we now have, it is very much in use in the tarot readings. The last card, which is the 22nd card, is the World card.

There are some packs where cards numbered 8 and 11 are transposed and Justice appears as 11 and Strength as 8, and some, like mine are not numbered at all. It is therefore essential to learn using the names of the cards rather than the numbers upon them. Those who are interested in the history of the cards may be interested to learn that the surviving trump cards from the fifteenth century are, in the main, unnumbered, and the original or proper sequence of the cards and their numbers is open to conjecture. The cards of the major arcana represent the physical and spiritual side of mankind. They can also refer to actual events or planetary influences. In many cases they can also be the story of a myth or legend.

I always explain the major arcana as a man on a journey, similar to John Bunyan's Pilgrim's Progress, or to Chaucer's Canterbury Tales. He (the Fool) starts on a road and meets people as he travels, coming to the end of his journey a little more enlightened, complete or fulfilled (the World). This can be both a physical and spiritual journey, and it is important to stress this dual aspect.

I always say to people that the minor arcana represents probable events or what is happening now, and the major arcana represents reasons behind the events, the more spiritual side of life.

Over the years that I have been using tarot cards, I have noticed that most people seem somewhat taken aback by a few of the major arcana cards, due to their illustrations and names, so I will state here and now that the cards called Hermit, Hanged Man, Death and Devil are nothing to be afraid of. Many people see the illustration for Death, for example, see the word Death, and assume it means that they are going to be killed in a road crash or something equally terrible. This is not the case; as we go through the meanings of the major arcana, you will see that there really is nothing to fear from these cards.

Those interested in numerology may care to note that the Death card is usually numbered 13, considered by many to be an unlucky number, and supposedly linked with there having been 13 at the Last Supper.

Each of the major arcana cards show a symbolic picture, illustrating in some way the name of the card concerned. This combination of illustration and name helps the beginner with the interpretation of the card.

In order to give you an initial understanding of the major arcana, I will list below the main names for the cards in sequence, with their French and Italian counterparts. The numerals here are in the English form, but you will notice that on most sets of cards, the numbers are Roman numerals, with 4 shown as IIII, rather than IV, 9 shown as VIIII, and 19 as XVIIII.

Card No.	Card Name
	THE FOOL; LE MAT; IL MATTO
1	THE MAGICIAN, JUGGLER; BATELEUR; BAGATTO
2	THE HIGH PRIESTESS; JUNON, LA PAPESSE; LA PAPESSA
3	THE EMPRESS; L'IMPERATRICE
4	THE EMPEROR; L'EMPEREUR; L'IMPERATORE
5	THE HEIROPHANT, POPE, JUPITER; LE PAPE; IL PAPA
6	THE LOVERS; L' AMOUREUX; GLI AMANTI
7	THE CHARIOT; LE CHARIOT; IL CARRO
8	JUSTICE; LA JUSTICE; LA GUISTIZIA
9	THE HERMIT, THE OLD MAN; L'ERMITE; L'ERMITA
10	THE WHEEL OF FORTUNE; LA ROUE DE FORTUNE; ROTA DI FORTUNA
11	STRENGTH, FORCE, FORTITUDE; LA FORCE; LA FORZA
12	THE HANGED MAN OR HANGING MAN, THE TRAITOR; LE PENDU, IL PENDUTO
13	DEATH; LA MORT; IL MORTE
14	TEMPERANCE; LA TEMPERANCE; LA TEMPERANZA
15	THE DEVIL; LE DIABLE; IL DIAVOLO
16	THE TOWER, LIGHTNING-STRUCK TOWER, HOUSE OF GOD, TOWER OF BABEL; LA MAI SON DE DIEU; LA TORRE
17	THE STAR; L'ETOILE; LA STELLE
18	THE MOON; LA LUNE; LA LUNA
19	THE SUN; LE SOLEIL; IL SOLE
20	JUDGEMENT, LAST JUDGEMENT; LE JUGEMENT; L'ANGELO
21	THE WORLD, UNIVERSE; LE MONDE; IL MONDO

Interpreting the Cards

When setting about interpreting the cards, it is important to look at the way the cards lie when dealt on to the table, as you may find some are upside-down or *inverted*. This will mean that the actual meaning of the card will be either weakened or sometimes even reversed, and as we go through the meanings of the cards, we will also discuss the inverted meanings. However, some tarot readers may feel differently about the meanings of the cards when inverted. Some say that as the minor arcana cards, with the exception of the court cards, have neither a right nor wrong way up it is impossible to give a weakened meaning.

The other thing to remember when using the cards is the way they lie together. I always say to people that your life is like a book, and while we may look at a couple of pages or more, it is the overall story that is important, and not necessarily the individual pages, so look at how the cards relate one to another, and read them as a whole, not as a series of cards which may seem disjointed.

When doing a full reading using all the tarot cards, you may notice that there are a lot of twos in the cards, or a lot of swords. This should be taken into account, as well as whether the cards are upside-down (inverted) or not. The card number or suits which dominate a reading are known as the *primary majority,* whereas the next largest suit or set of numbers is known as the *secondary majority.* These can tell us things of personal concern as well as about external events.

It is important to remember at all times that what will be seen in the cards will be a trend, and possibilities will be given rather than definite solutions or events. Everyone has free will; whatever is said to them, they remain free to choose their own route rather than the one outlined to them. That is what makes us all individuals. The destination may be fixed, but the route to it is not. It is important to make this point clear when consulting the cards for others.

As we near the end of the book, we will discuss some of the many and varied types of spread, and actually go through a sample reading, so you can get the idea of how the cards relate to each other.

We should always try to make our subject feel at ease, as it is much more fun and a lot easier to do readings for people who are in a relaxed and happy frame of mind than for those who are sceptical or tense, or who have rushed to get to you - a reading produced under such circumstances will most likely be confused and unsatisfactory. It is important to emphasise that tarot readings, whilst they can be fun, are not a game, and those who wrap their cards up in silk or keep them special in some way will already have accepted this fact and take the question of reading tarot cards seriously.

Never force a card reading on to someone, even if you are desperate to show off your newly acquired reading skills; likewise make sure that both you and the person consulting the cards have serious . intent. I have known of people, who are just playing with the cards, come up with the most bizarre reading, which makes no sense whatsoever. Some people only use the 22 major arcana cards. When I am doing a personal sitting, I more often than not use playing cards, which correspond in the main to the minor arcana, for part of the reading and the major arcana for the other part, using the full tarot pack only in postal readings or when specifically requested. However, how you use the cards will be a personal thing for you. You may look at the spreads and devise one of your own, which is what I did, or you may decide to use one of the conventional spreads on a regular basis. It is entirely up to you, and will depend upon what you feel comfortable doing.

Before going on, be sure that you acquire a set of your own cards (if you haven't already got a pack), which you should look through and familiarise yourself with, as they will be needed for all your future work.

PRACTICE

At the end of each chapter we will have a short question section, without answers, for you to start to think a little more about what has been discussed. As we have just been looking at the major and minor arcana, the questions are based on these.

- How many cards are there in the full tarot pack?
- How many cards are numbered in the major arcana?
- How many suits are there in the minor arcana, and how do these cards differ from the cards in the standard playing card pack?
- Does the Fool card come at the start of the major arcana or at the start of the minor arcana?

CHAPTER 2 – THE Major Arcana

The word arcana actually means secret, but during the course of this 1book, we will endeavour, to uncover the meanings of the tarot cards, both major and minor, in upright and reversed (inverted) positions.

As we have already established, the major arcana comprises 22 cards and we have seen their names, in more than one language, and their numbers.

You should have your own cards ready at this point, and as we go through, refer to the illustrations on your own set of cards (which may differ from the descriptions given here).

Other Links

Each of the cards will concern both the material and spiritual, and indicate steps necessary towards self-knowledge.

There is a close relationship between the cards and astrology and numerology, and where appropriate, information will be given to link these. However, please note that with the astrological link there could be several possible orders for the seven planets, and some writers, who base their conclusions on what are known as the essential dignities, have arrived at different planetary associations than those listed here, which are modern interpretations. These modern interpretations are no less effective than the essential dignities but are merely another viewpoint

The Meaning of Cards

The Fool

The unnumbered card, and the card which became the Joker in the standard playing cards. When drawing the Fool in any spread, we should expect the unexpected. Things may not go according to plan, and new opportunities and new horizons will be offered. This could be a fresh start or a change of attitude on our part, leading to sometimes surprising discoveries. The Fool card marks the start of the journey of self discovery, and can indicate nervousness, foolishness, naivety, immaturity and lack of willpower and discipline. It can, however, also indicate confidence, fun and idealism. The Fool suggests new beginnings, a new start, or even a new way of looking at an old problem, being careful, however, not to be foolish when faced with choices. We are being urged to move forward, to start a new chapter, maybe impulsively, and tackle something new, perhaps despite our conscious mind. Should the card be reversed, there may be wrong choices made and the new start may be delayed, possibly due to our own apathy. We are also warned against taking unnecessary risks or gambles.

The card relates to the planet Uranus, the planet of independence and change - breaking away and making new starts. As stated earlier, the card is unnumbered. In ancient times, the concept of zero did not exist, and in numerological terms zero is meaningless.

The Magician

Numbered 1, in most packs the Magician will be seen with the symbols of the pentacles, swords, cups and wands around him or as part of the illustration. These are the suits of the minor arcana. To be a successful magician, one must be original, and this is a key word in the meaning of the card. Imagination, skill, dexterity and also deception are indicated. Again choices are to be made, and there are indications that the magician, with his skills, is there to guide us. We are warned not to be inflexible, and to look at our own powers and skills, perhaps hidden or unused, and not to rely on others to help us through. We should promote ourselves, be determined and prepared for change, and look for opportunities to use our talents to their full potential in the future. Should the card be reversed, lack of imagination and drive may well hold up any progress. It is also possible that the talents uncovered may not be used wisely or well. There is an insecurity or lack of faith stopping our progress. We should also watch for trickery. Strength of mind is required.

The card is said to link with the planet Mercury, the unconscious communicating with the conscious, the psyche communicating with the conscious mind. In numerology, number 1 normally connects with the Sun, and is a strong number, the number of will, drive, ambition and self.

The High Priestess

Numbered 2, this card represents wisdom, in its female form. Common sense, inherent knowledge and intuition are all part of its meaning. It can also indicate psychic or artistic abilities of which we may not be totally aware, but of which our inner-self has full knowledge. This card suggests mystery and secrets; our powers of intuition and insight will be heightened, and we will be helped by our own psyche. Changes may be quite dramatic. We may develop a leaning towards things of an esoteric nature, and find ourselves teaching or helping others. This card is essentially a learning card. Should the card be reversed, we are warned to watch our, emotions and mood swings, to let go of negativities. There is ignorance around us and we are likely to be deceived by those who can see a potential victim in us. There is also a warning, if the card is in the reversed position, for us to guard against being selfish, unforgiving, careless or excessive.

In ancient times, the high priestess was also called the Moon Goddess, and therefore the card links with the Moon, which in turn links with instinct, emotions, reflection and, ultimately, change. In numerology number 2 is the number of duality, imagination and harmony.

The Empress

Numbered 3, this card represents feminine accomplishment and achievement, love, beauty and fertility. The Empress has improved her circumstances by using wisdom and strength, as well as her creativity. This card can herald births, weddings, house moves or changes. It does not necessarily follow, however, that the experience of mothering will be ours in a literal sense, but that we can bring something to fruition. The need for harmony will be strong, as will the need for love and affection. Emotional security will be high on the list of priorities at this time. Projects are likely to reach fruition when this card is drawn and plans will be fulfilled. This is a card of action and desire. Should the card be reversed, we are warned against indecision, lack of creativity and concentration, delay, waste and inaction. We are also warned that there are possible domestic upheavals awaiting us, maybe also monetary worries, due to our hesitancy, anxiety and inaction. We are warned against controlling situations through being unable to let go.

The card links with Venus, and especially Taurus, therefore with unity, balance and materialism. Number 3 in numerology links with Jupiter, and is the number of the ambitious, yet extremely conscientious individual. As it links to the number 9, which is a special number, it is said to balance the spirit with the mind and the body.

The Emperor

Numbered 4, this card again represents worldly power and ambition, but is masculine in leadership, logic and power. The Emperor is a wealthy man, sitting on his throne, and has persevered and been assertive to realise his goals. This is now seen as being necessary to the person drawing this card. He is the King of his country, of his realm. His position is unassailable and stable. He has followed his convictions and dominated his foes. He is also the father figure, as he is the father of his country, in the same way as his wife, the Empress, is the mother of her country. He suggests to us that we must not let emotion and passion lead us astray; intelligence and reason must win through. He is someone we can trust, who can be seen as a good friend to us when in need. Knowledge may come from someone we see as influential. He heralds improvements, but only if we choose to act. Should the card be reversed, we are warned that there are those around us who are not what they appear, and we must not be weak willed or immature; nor should we be proud, cold, unfeeling or selfish. The card could also indicate a dislike of authority figures and rules - a rebellious streak in our nature. The card links with Mars, and especially with Aries.

The number 4 links with Uranus, the number of the rebel, the person who seeks reform and change but is positive and strong, yet can alienate himself from others, and become distant.

The Hierophant

Numbered 5, this card represe.nts mystery, psychic awareness, inner WIsdom, spiritual power, and the spiritual quest. We are looking for answers within, and may look to other philosophies for our answers. The Hierophant is the kind, generous teacher and confidant. He can also be a person dealing with the psyche, a priest or a spiritual guide. He tells us that what we seek will come, maybe through an alliance, but we may have to be patient. He shows kindness and compassion. Drawing this card warns us to guard against anything unkind, illegal or immoral, as what we do must be seen to be right by our creator. We cannot totally follow the physical path. Like the Emperor, here is someone to whom we can turn in trouble, but someone who will understand the emotional side of our nature. Sometimes drawing this card can indicate a person of religious or spiritual nature. Should the card be reversed, we are warned against being over kind or generous, as this would indeed be foolish on our part. There is a vulnerability against which we should guard. We should be careful to stick to the traditional path, and not try anything unconventional, unspiritual, rebellious or unorthodox.

This card is said to link with Jupiter, also with Pisces. In numerology, the number 5 links with Mercury, and suggests friendliness, quick thought and action, and versatility.

The lovers

Numbered 6, this card is the card of choice. There may be a problem with relationships versus job or hobby, of there being a choice concerning more than one lover, or a duality in another sense, as in our relationship with ourself, or even a hasty marriage which proves unwise. Whatever the case, choices are necessary, and the decisions made are crucial. We seek compatibility, romance, and perfection, but will be put to the test and examined. This card can herald the start of a new romance or a struggle with an existing relationship. Through this set of circumstances, however, we will learn more about ourselves. Choices made should be guided by our inner self, rather than logic..We should guard against temptations placed in front of us and listen more to our inner wisdom. This card can also indicate the need to spend money on a project or on another person. Should the card be reversed, unwise plans, wrong choices, fickleness and separation, or infidelity are suggested.

This card is said to have links with Mercury and with Gemini, the sign of duality. In numerology, the number 6 links with Venus. Six is the number of magnetism, attraction and love, and determination to succeed despite all odds.

The Chariot

Numbered 7, the Chariot card is the card of movement, challenge and conquest, but not without ordeal and trouble, from which we will emerge all the stronger. It can herald changes at work or at home, and as it shows a mode of transport, it can warn of trouble with transport or movement of some sort. It can also indicate that we might encounter aggression from others. We are aiming for success, but it will not come without effort on our part. We must watch our emotions, be disciplined, and be in control of the situations with which we are faced. However, we must also recognise our own inner wisdom, and listen to it if we are to succeed, regulating our competitive instincts. There will be times when we have to balance our work with pleasurable activities. Should the card be reversed, we may face defeat or be unsuccessful in our endeavours due to our inability to face reality and lack of strength. This card is said to have links with the Moon, and with Cancer in particular. In numerology, 7 traditionally links with Neptune, and relates to the spiritual, mystic or mysterious force. It does however link with the Moon in as much as 2 is a secondary number of 7. Seven is the number of cycles, and as it links with Sunday (the 7th day) has associations with rest and relaxation. As 7 is made up of the numbers 3 (with spiritual links) and 4 (with rebellious material links), it is also said to join body and soul together.

Justice

Numbered 8 in most packs, this card represents balance, moderation and fairness. It has obvious legal connotations and may warn of legal matters entering our lives, such as contracts or papers. It can be seen as a marriage contract, a reunion, or even a political stance. The scales are balanced, and there is a need for balance and order in our lives. Decisions are to be made, and good advice may be given to us, which we should weigh up and reflect upon before acting. We must not, however, be indecisive or put the blame on to others for our own shortcomings. We need to be sensible, impartial and virtuous.

The card indicates hopes and fears balanced against morals, and is the first of the four moral lesson cards, the others being Temperance, Strength and the Hermit. This card indicates the building of our character. We need a balanced mind to resolve problems of any nature, and we are being told to seek that balance. Should the card be reversed, we may suffer falseness, abuse, bigotry or unfairness in some way. Legal action undertaken may prove costly and financial loss may result. We may also be suffering from a lack of perspective.

In astrological terms, the card has obvious links with Libra, the scales. The number 8 links with Saturn, and represents two worlds interlinking, the spiritual and the material, and is traditionally associated with fate, philosophical matters, upheaval and concentration of purpose.

The Hermit

Numbered 9, the Hermit shows a need for retreat within, a period of solitude or isolation, during which we can deliberate and think things through. Any study undertaken at this time is likely to be successful, as the card indicates wisdom and progress. Shrewd thinking can help us in our spiritual growth, and we may now find ourselves reading a great deal, or even attending evening classes in relaxation or meditation. The card is associated with the spiritual quest, the inner search, through meditation, self-denial and reflection. We must be prudent, patient and cautious, and now is the time to consider long-term plans in order to feel settled.

There is a need to reassess before proceeding further. This may result in our leaving a situation in order to be on our own, or we may be forced to be on our own. It can also indicate old age or old people and the passing of time, from youth to maturity and into old age. Should the card be reversed, we are warned against hasty actions, rashness, or childish behaviour. We may be surrounded by unreasonable doubts or suffer from self-deception or delay.

The card is said to link with Mercury and Virgo in particular, and in numerological terms, 9 links with Mars and represents man, the physical and material plane, being the number of force and energy. Nine is an indestructible number.

The Wheel of Fortune

Numbered 10, this card signifies progress, the end of a cycle, promotion, progress, luck (good or bad), sudden change and new things. It is also associated with money, the Wheel of Fortune being associated with the roulette wheel. However, there is the element of chance involved, so any changes may not be what we expect. Some people call this fate. We must learn to let go of the past to progress. The changes anticipated when drawing this card could be related to work, home, relationships or lifestyle.

This is a card of expansion. We must realise, however, that the wheel will roll onwards, and what was the top of the wheel may soon become the bottom, so things must not be taken for granted. Good luck and success can easily turn to bad luck and ruin, but we must be optimistic that fate will not deal us a cruel hand, nor will our inner-self, if listened to, lead us astray. We must continue to consult our own wisdom, and pursue our inner journey of discovery. The card symbolises our desires in material as well as spiritual matters. Should the card be reversed, we may face failure, anxiety, inconsistencies, delays or stagnation. Events may not turn out as we hoped.

The card is connected with Jupiter and the changing of cycles. In numerology, 10 becomes one, and the cycle of 1-9 starts all over again. It is the number of eternity, of the universe, rise and fall, but ultimately of self-confidence.

Strength

Numbered 11 in most packs, this card signifies the need for courage, energy, determination, strength of character and purpose, confidence and self-reliance. We must be determined if we want to succeed. It tells us to put our plans into action with courage and strength of mind. The card can also indicate a recovery from illness; strength has returned, both in mind and body. There is no further need for tools with which to attack the problem, as we can do this now unaided. We must have the courage of our convictions. We must also face our faults, acknowledge their existence and do something positive to lessen their impact on our lives. As the card represents spiritual as well as physical strength, we may be aware of hidden forces at work, seeming to help us through. We may have to overcome material pursuits and selfish inclinations, and focus a little more on the spiritual side of ourselves. Should the card be reversed, we are warned to tread carefully, watch loneliness, overtiredness, bad temper or illness. We may suffer a lack of faith; discord and weakness could surround us. We must be sure to use any power wisely and avoid being overbearing.

Astrologically, the card has links with Leo, the lion. In numerology, 11 is a master number, one of mystical significance. It represents a need to contend with difficulties. It is also sometimes called the number of sins, representing the struggle between vice and virtue.

The Hanged Man

Numbered 12, this card seems to frighten most people, probably due to its illustration. It basically shows the need to adapt to changes in order to find inner space. We are unable to do a great deal to alter our circumstances. However, we must try to make adjustments and sacrifices in order to gain the improvement we seek. This has to be voluntary and understood. We may feel trapped, anxious, fearful, and be unable to move forward, but we may also be sitting on the fence, either emotionally or in a material sense, awaiting changes which will allow us more freedom. The card indicates we may have to sacrifice something we consider important in order to move forward and develop. In the same way as the perspective of the man and his view of life have changed, so must ours. Our spirituality will be increasing, and we may have to make material sacrifices. We are undergoing an expansion of consciousness. Should the card be reversed, we may be looking for escape, and be preoccupied with self. Falseness and lack of effort on our part will prevent our moving forward. We must make the effort if we are to progress.

This card is associated with Neptune, linking inspiration with the conscious mind. Twelve is associated with the 12 Disciples and with sacrifice, suffering and anxiety, but also with grace and perfection.

Death

Numbered 13, this card again has a frightening effect when appearing in a spread, but should not be seen as an actual death but as the death of a situation, sudden change, the resolution of problems. There is a need to move on which must be recognised. People or things may want to hold you back but you must realise that this cannot happen. There may be partings indicated by the card, better health, and possible failures. It suggests the end of a phase and moving on to pastures new; we cannot cling to the past. Part of our old self has to die if we are to complete the transformation we ,- . want. The changes required might be drastic. There could be a need for a new attitude, new surroundings, new challenges, new relationships. There may be a new child in our lives, a new marriage, a new job. Things will change; a lifestyle may die. We must accept this. Should the card be reversed, changes may be partial. There may be immobility, anger, boredom, depression, illness or loss. We will recover, but the change will be slow.

This card is associated with Pluto and rebirth. The number 13, whilst considered unlucky, is really a number of power when used correctly but, if used wrongly, it will destroy itself. It is the number of the unknown or unexpected. The reason for it being considered unlucky lies with there having been 13 at the Last Supper.

Temperance

Numbered 14, this card shows the need to control forces if harmony is to be achieved. We must be patient, self-controlled and calm. The card also represents a strong ally or friend, a possible reconciliation, and the need for rest to maintain good health. We must be balanced, diplomatic, and exercise moderation in our lives, especially when dealing with other people. There is a need for exchange, possibly of communication, in a relationship. We must assess our feelings. Patience is something we must acquire, as restlessness and wasting of energy will leave us depleted. This is a card of regeneration. The drawing of this card can indicate a need for economies to be made, which may be either financial or emotional. Changes will occur which will be good for us, and we may recoup things which we had previously thought lost to us. Others will be helpful to us and we could find ourselves in a good partnership situation. Should the card be reversed, we will be faced with discord, conflict and unfulfilled desires, possibly due to our own stubbornness and inactivity. There is a fickleness around us, hostility and lack of patience.

This card has links with Jupiter, and Sagittarius in particular. In numerology, 14 is the number of caution and risk. It also has Biblical links, as Jesus was said to have been sacrificed for humanity on the 14th day of the first month.

The Devil

Numbered 15, again this card tends to alarm those who are unaware of the meaning behind the illustration. The card suggests enslavement, subordination and, ultimately, self-punishment, and warns that we must not allow ourselves to become someone's puppet. The card can refer to obligations from which we should disentangle ourselves, and suggests hidden forces at work against which we should be prepared. We should also be careful of any physical excesses of any kind, excessive materialism and over-indulgence.

We must let go of outworn or outmoded ideals and do something positive to alter those aspects of our personality which do not fit in with our ultimate goal for ourselves. As the devil is traditionally associated with the material and physical side of man, it can suggest that more money will be at our disposal, but we must watch how this is used. We could be offered a business partnership of some description, but again this should be carefully reflected upon before any decisions are made, as we could become enslaved. Should the card be reversed, we should watch for animosity and our own stupidity. We may find that we will overcome handicaps and our own anxieties, thus making it easier to continue our quest for spirituality.

This card links with Mars and also with Capricorn. In numerology, the number 15 is a number of great significance, of magic and mystery, for baser reasons rather than for spiritual purposes. It is always considered a lucky number for those seeking extra money.

The Tower

Numbered 16, this card shows disruption, setbacks, some suffering due to natural causes, and, again, is a card which tends to cause concern to those finding it in a spread. The card heralds a new era. When • the Tower falls, whether the cause is external, internal, or a combination of the two reasons, it is possible to rebuild using the old bricks and arrive at a new and possibly better building. Things may happen suddenly,
but hope should remain at all costs. Changes could be apparent at home, in relationships or at work, and a loss of security could result, but this will ultimately be for the best. The card could mean bankruptcy or extreme financial loss, but we will learn and grow from the experience. Old forms collapse and new forms take their place. Such is progress. Maybe there is a need for us to adopt a new approach, and it is the old attitudes which will fall. This card need not necessarily herald a calamity in the physical sense, but a mental progression. If we are being false in some way, we must now face this, and change. The collapse of the Tower is inevitable; we must come to terms with this and any confusion it brings. Should the card be reversed, we may find ourselves in an untenable situation, oppressed or unhappy. We are warned to watch for lies, both our own and those of others.

Astrologically, the card has links with Mars but also connects with Mercury. In numerology, the number 16 tells of accidents, danger and fatality.

The Star

Numbered 17, this card is the card of hope. It points the way to an easier existence, providing we have faith, hope and trust. It heralds good fortune, better situations, good news, rest and relaxation, satisfaction and also a period of study in order for knowledge to grow. This card is the card of new life, talents and vigour. We should learn to guard against our self-doubts and have faith, trusting in our own inner wisdom and strengths. The Star card has links with the Star of Bethlehem, which served as a guide to those seeking the Messiah, and should be similarly regarded by those looking at the tarot pack, in that we will be guided and must have hope in a happy outcome. We will find redemption and salvation, but should beware of sinking into baser values and becoming dependent upon others. Our hope should not be blind, however. Should the card be reversed, we may fall victim to a spell of bad luck or pessimism, not seizing opportunities presented, making errors of judgement through weakness or stress. We are warned that some of our friendships may not be beneficial to us, despite current harmonious situations.

Astrologically, this card links with Aquarius, the water-bearer, but also with Venus. Numerologically, 17 is a number of immortality, connecting to 8 which in turn connects with the 8-pointed Star of Venus. Often 17 is connected with people whose names live on after them.

The Moon

Numbered 18, this card is a card of reflection, rest and intuition. It is the card of the unconscious. We are becoming aware of our hidden depths. There will be uncertainty around us in our dealings with ourselves and with others. We may be subject to changing moods, which may or may not actually fall in with the changing cycles of the moon. It warns of trickery, double-dealing, dishonesty and deception, false friends and hidden dangers. However, it can also herald changes for the good, despite any insincerities or naivety associated with ourselves or others. We must learn to rely on ourselves, not worry and be firm. The card sometimes has connections with show business ventures. The card traditionally links heaven, hell and earth, and can be seen as a crossroads, with choices offered. Should the card be reversed, we should read the small print in any contracts or legal documents, overcome worries or insecurities and learn to rely on ourselves and our own judgement. Astrologically, the card links with the Moon and also with Pisces. Numerologically, the number 18 is symbolic of materialism making endeavours to destroy spirituality, and is connected with quarrels and upsets, treachery and deception.

The Sun

Numbered 19, this card is the light of the higher self. It is also the card for the life-force of the earth, as without the light and heat from the sun, the earth would be no more. It is the card of safety after a period of strain and stress, wealth, money, travel, pleasure and good friendships. Our health will improve, we will feel energetic and have more self-confidence and self-worth. It can herald a period of intense creativity and happiness. We will have clarity of mind and action and will move forward, having found the right course. We have foresight, purpose and the energy to carry out our desires. We are nearing the end of a long tunnel and can see our way forward. Should this card be drawn by a person about to be married, it portends a happy marriage and a devoted partner. It also is a card of promotion and success in job related matters. Should the card be reversed, we are warned against materialism, and must be cautious that our power-drive and push do not lead to our ultimately being lonely and unhappy. Arrogance is something which we should guard against. Plans may be changed and we should proceed with caution.

Astrologically, the card links with the sun and with Aries, the first sign of the zodiac and a new cycle. Numerologically, the number 19 promises happiness and success.

Judgement

Numbered 20, and also called Last Judgement, this card is a return to health, a new lease of life, a rebirth, change and readjustment. Improvements will be apparent in all our dealings and again promotion or job successes could result. We will find our spirituality reawakening; things we felt to no longer be a part of our lives, especially creative or spiritual interests, will re-emerge, and a new creativity be around us. The changes may not be material, as the emphasis here is on spirituality and ultimate fulfilment. We may find ourselves rewarded for past efforts, but we may also find things we had suppressed reasserting themselves in our lives. This is a new chapter, an awakening of a higher consciousness, and forgiveness of mistakes and failures. We must learn, and should have now realised, the need to be true to ourselves. Should the card be reversed, we must guard against failure to face facts, and delay and obstacles being placed in our path. We should be prepared to move forward and not wait for things to go right for us. The card can sometimes means divorce or separation.

Astrologically, the card has links with Pluto, which signifies success in a spiritual sense. Numerologically, the number 20 is an awakening of new purpose, plans and ambitions, but as it is not a wordly number, does not link with material concerns. It concerns the development of spirituality.

The World

Numbered 21, and the last of the trump cards, the World - is the summation of all the cards which have gone before. It is the completion of the cycle of self-knowledge, yet the cycle is not ended, as we will continue on our journey of improvement, wiser for what has gone before. We have now learnt both material and spiritual lessons and should we face similar problems and hardships again, we will be wiser for the lessons we have learnt. This card is the card of favourable changes, happiness, travel, moves and enjoyment of the results of our efforts. Where we have ended, another journey will begin. Whenever we feel we have reached our aims and our goals, it is time to set new targets and strive for new challenges. We will forever move forward. This is a card of good fortune. Should the card be reversed, we may find we have given up half-way through a project or a situation which could have been resolved. We have suffered a lack of vision and incentive, due to immaturity. We are warned to watch legal matters. This is also a card, which, when reversed, indicates someone who is deeply shy and who needs to be more confident and outgoing. It can also show a dislike of change and fear of happiness.

Astrologically, the card links with Saturn, and with Libra. Nurnerologically, this number means victory after a battle, advancement and appreciation.

Practice

This chapter's questions revolve around the major arcana.

- What, in brief terms, is the meaning of the Death card in its upright position?
- What card normally ends the major arcana cards?
- Does the Devil card indicate someone is likely to be possessed by evil?
- In general terms, what difference is there in meanings between an upright and reversed Hermit card?
- Does the Lover card indicate a romance?
- How would you explain the meaning of the Justice card?
- Which card indicates the start of a journey of discovery?

CHAPTER 3 – The Suite of the Swords

The Minor Arcana

In the last chapter we concentrated solely on the major arcana, and there has been a lot to learn. Having mastered the major arcana, we are now moving on to the minor arcana, and in this and the next three chapters we will cover the suits of swords, wands, cups and pentacles. These suits contain 14 cards each and there are therefore only 14 cards per chapter to concentrate upon. We will start with the suit of swords.

Brief, General Meanings

As we have already established, the suit of swords corresponds to the spades in a standard pack of playing cards. They also represent the executive classes, the element of air, and mental matters. As we progress through the meanings of each card, we will also link hair colourings, zodiac signs, personality types etc. to the court or picture cards in each suit. In general terms, Kings and Queens of whatever suit usually represent people rather than situations, but this is not a hard and fast rule. Please note that some authors will link swords to the element of fire . and wands to the element of air. This is open to conjecture. Also, not every reader will have a reverse meaning for the pip cards (those cards numbered 2 to 10). The reverse meanings will be given here, but it is up to each individual reader to determine for themselves whether these cards have a right or wrong way to face. It is obvious, for example, when a court card is upside-down, but this is not always so with the pip cards. The decision is therefore yours, and I would suggest you try both methods for a while before making any firm decisions, one way or another.

In general terms, swords, also called epees, represent action, progress - either good or bad, ambition, opposition, authority and strength. Swords generally indicate there is, or will be, a problem which requires action. Swords can also often indicate health concerns or problems. People represented by the suit of swords are decisive, professional people.

The Meaning of the Cards

Kings of swords

This card represents an active man, a warrior and leader of his country. He has experience and has learnt how to control himself and his emotions. He is used to dealing in strategy and is analytical by nature. He tends to represent a professional person, and will generally be either very dark or very fair in colouring, tall and slim, with a thin face and sharp features. He is seemingly unemotional and logical. It is often the case, however, that there is a vulnerability beneath the hard exterior presented to the world. Often this card can represent a lawyer, soldier or doctor. This man does not act on impulse but can be impatient and always thinks of himself as being correct in everything he does. He suggests the need to look to new ideas and embark on a project, and can herald sudden promotion or advancement, or help from someone in a high position. Should the card be reversed, this is a person who will stop at nothing to achieve his aims, and can often fail as a result. This is a selfish person, someone without any scruples. We are warned to look out for such a person in a professional capacity.

The Queen of Swords

This card represents a quick-thinking, and often sharp-tongued, woman. She could be a widow, or someone on her own and lonely. She is someone who knows what it is like to have no companion in life, having had happy times in the past, but now experiencing sadness and misery. Her colouring and features will be similar to those of the King. She is often talented or creative, steadfast in all her endeavours, and someone who commands respect. She suggests the need to adopt similar characteristics of strength of purpose, or that we will be helped by someone with these qualities. Should the card be reversed, we are warned against narrow mindedness, ill-temper or deceit. The card also links with loss of some kind, either personal or emotional. It is possible that we will be meeting someone with lesser qualities, perhaps a lady.

Knight of Swords

An intuitive and imaginative person, very much like flan Aquarius in nature, always wanting new and untried ways of doing things and disliking the traditional paths, this person may get easily bored and be forever changing direction. However, his intentions are good and honourable, and he never means to cause distress or hurt by his actions. He has no fear of the unknown, is brave and heroic. He suggests that we need similar qualities. He can also herald a change of home or a sudden need to change jobs and tackle something previously untried. Changes will, perhaps, be too sudden. As the Knight is fearless, his presence suggests that we be equally fearless and unemotional. Should the card be reversed, we are warned to watch impulsive actions, as they could prove costly. There could be problems with relationships with a lady; we should be careful not to be conceited in our dealings with others. There may be health or legal matters which need attention.

Page of Swords

This young person is very discerning, sporting, active and intelligent. He seems to possess the quality of insight and is discreet in his own dealings. The presence of this card suggests the help of such a person, unexpected help in financial matters and success in business, or the need to adopt such qualities. We are to watch out for opportunities, contracts and help. Should the card be reversed, illness is suggested. We may be subject to delays, due to lack of preparation or the interference of someone who was out to cause us problems from the start, although we perhaps did not see this at the time. This person could be quite childish and slanderous. It is possible that we may have problems with an aggressive child.

Ace of Swords

This is the card of determination, will-power and justice. It shows the need to meet a situation head-on, and change is inevitable. We must act with integrity and firmness in order to win through. We will need all our powers of concentration. We may find ourselves acting with a passion and determination seldom encountered before. Should the card be reversed, there will be delays in starting new projects, I 'l or health or emotional problems which will delay our start. We should watch for clashes with figures of authority, disruption and apathy. We should be careful that flashes of temper do not cause more trouble than anticipated.

Two of Swords

This is a card of harmony, but also of stalemate and lack of movement. Maybe we ourselves are reluctant to make the necessary changes, refusing to see the obvious. The change will happen eventually, and we should just face this. Any rifts may be resolved and we will earn the respect of those around us, as this is also a card of affection. Should the card be reversed, we have false friends and people are not being honest with us, or maybe we are lying ourselves. We could face problems due to other people not being what they seem, and clashes with authority are again indicated. However, the stalemate will end, things will start to move and we will feel more able to deal with the situation.

Three of Swords

This is a card of loss of possessions, health or friendships. This is the time to try to sort out problems, but we should be prepared for delay and disappointments. We cannot be self-deluding. What we are encountering is necessary for us to progress, but it is not an easy time. Should the card be reversed, any illness or loss may be minor or less traumatic for us and we are more able to get on with life. We may find ourselves seeking a period of seclusion and may feel confused, sad or alone. This card can indicate a period of separation from loved ones and a feeling of incompatibility.

Four of Swords

This card is the card of rest and recovery from emotional or physical problems. There is a need for meditation and reflection, to recharge our batteries. Often this card suggests a period where we will be alone and need to be alone. However, we can also feel abandoned by others. This card sometimes indicates a stay in hospital. Should the card be reversed, any isolation may be forced upon us. Often the card can suggest a period of incarceration or exile. We may feel the need to recover things we thought lost; we will recover financial losses, albeit slowly. We may feel restricted, helpless and lost, but things will improve.

Five of Swords

We realise we cannot run away forever and must stand and face up to our problems, limitations and responsibilities. Partings may occur; someone may even leave the country, leaving us sad and sorrowful, but new starts are also indicated. We should watch for trouble-makers, violence and arguments. We will win through in the end, although our reputation may be tarnished. We should guard against taking on too much and being unable to cope. Should the card be reversed, the problems encountered above will be less stressful. We should, however, watch for possible theft, and guard our possessions.

Six of Swords

A visit overseas is likely, and any such journey will be profitable. Anxieties will be resolved; we are moving from stormy seas into a lake of tranquillity. We have learnt from our problems and have peace of mind. The card can often herald marriage proposals, and we will feel free and happy. We may have visitors from abroad, or we may even be moving ourselves. Should the card be reversed, any proposal may be unwanted, and the situation will be seemingly slow to improve. Journeys will face delays, and we should watch our finances. In any legal matters, the outcome may not be in our favour. We may suffer poor health as a result of stress.

Seven of Swords

A card of confidence, hope and faith. We will be receiving business or legal advice, which will be wise and we should follow. This is a card of ambition and effort. New plans, hopes and aims are coming; we must have confidence in a good outcome, persevere and be patient. We should use our tact in difficult situations, and although we may feel we are not being true to ourselves, it is necessary to act in this way to secure a good result. Should the card be reversed, we will face disappointments, quarrels and advice given may not be sound. We should watch out for slander and loss. Things are going on which are not as they seem.

Eight of Swords

This is the end of a problematic time for us. We may feel restricted and unable to see how things can possibly improve, as conflict will still seem to be a major part of our life. As a result, we may be suffering stress-related problems. Wrongs will be righted, but in their time, not ours. We may fear the consequences of any actions. at this time and not want to cause trouble, but sometimes this is necessary. Should the card be reversed, restrictions will lift and setbacks be temporary, yet we should watch for accidents or financial loss. Any criticism at this time will be unwarranted. We may feel depressed and feel that fate is against us.

Nine of Swords

A card of illness and of loss. Sometimes these two are related. Recovery will be swift, however, and our faith renewed. We must be positive at all times, otherwise we will slide into despondency. Being fearful leads to its own problems, and we must look carefully at ourselves to see where faults lie. Family problems may surround us. This card sometimes suggests a miscarriage. Should the card be reversed, any miscarriage is likely to be a miscarriage of justice, and deception surrounds us. Anxiety and stress are apparent, and we may lose property or reputation. Rumours will abound; we may be worrying unnecessarily about our problems.

Ten of Swords

A situation is ending. This could mean a divorce, separation or other personal or emotional loss. The parting may not be what we want but it is necessary in order for new ideas and relationships to be formed or develop. There may be tears, grief and unhappiness. This is only temporary; things will improve. Any changes of this kind are difficult to cope with, but we do cope, and we come through the experience more positive and capable. Materially, a slight improvement is suggested, but we should still be watchful of other people, as deceit still surrounds us. Should the card be reversed, disappointments and setbacks will be minor. We may feel totally lost and a complete failure, but these feelings are purely emotional and not based on logic or reason. If we look at our lives more dispassionately, we will see that things are not really that bad. This is a card, when reversed, of profit and improvement.

Practice

The questions at the end of this chapter are based on the suit of swords.

- What do swords mean generally?
- What is the colouring normally associated with court cards from this suit?
- What does the two of swords indicate? Is there likely to be any change when this card appears?
- Someone has recently had health problems and draws the three of swords in their cards. Would this tally with these recent illnesses or not?
- What other cards in the suit of swords may turn up to indicate health problems?

CHAPTER 4 – The Suit of Wands

Brief, General Meanings

We have already established that wands, sometimes called sceptres, rods, batons or clubs, correspond to clubs in the standard pack of playing cards. We have also said that they generally correspond to lower income groups - hard-working, modest people, who are good company but may be unreliable. Wands represent challenge in all its forms and wand people are normally brown- or red-hatred and well built, energetic and restless. They correspond to the fire element. The appearance of wands in a spread means creativity, progress and growth through negotiation. Wands are generally optimistic cards but do not show the easy route.

The Meaning of the Cards

King of Wands

Good-looking, brown-hatred, well-built, honest and kindly, this is a mature person who is good with people, and often is representative of the teacher. He is very similar to the Heirophant in the major arcana, with some of the characteristics of the Emperor. He is a helpful sort of person, and although he may not always seem emotionally involved with the situation, is sympathetic and someone who can be turned to in a crisis for help or advice. He is wise and educated, and is a noble and strong leader. The appearance of the King of wands is a sign of moral and financial help. We must be as strong as he is to succeed, and we must believe in ourselves. He is a fatherly type of person and his advice is sound. Should the card be reversed, we are looking at a deceitful person, someone who will not offer advice or help. We are also looking at restrictions and losses.

Queen of Wands

A person who is popular in company and a graceful hostess, but also clever in business, with drive and enthusiasm. Sometimes a little rash, she is, like the King, sympathetic and understanding in a feminine way. She is extremely practical and clever, showing emotion and genuinely caring for those around her. Her surroundings are well balanced and harmonious. Her presence in a spread suggests we should try to attain similar qualities. It also suggests a good business venture will be put to us by a lady, and that anything to do with property or security is well favoured. Should the card be reversed, we are faced with a person who cannot really help us, despite the wish to do so. The lady may be untrustworthy or deceitful in some way, and her emotions (or ours) are not balanced. This is a card of opposition and also of fickleness and possible infidelities.

Knight of Wands

The presence of this card signifies travel and moves of some kind, which may be to do with residence or job, and be either temporary or permanent. We are moving into unknown areas. This could mean moving to live abroad. We may find ourselves easily bored and needing change for change's sake, without any real motive or purpose. As a person, the card represents .>'1 someone who is friendly, fearless, charming and intelligent yet rash and unreliable. This card often heralds meetings with people who work with people, such as teachers or social workers. Should the card be reversed, we are warned of insincerities and misunderstandings with those around us, leading to discord and friction. There may also be setbacks in journeys and changes, with things not going according to plan. There may be unfavourable events in personal relationships with possible separations resulting. Beware of taking others at face value.

Page of Wands

This is the true friend, the person who will stand by us, faithful and true, no matter what. The card can also be seen as a restless youngster. Often, the card can suggest meeting someone like this, who will herald the start of better times. We may hear or receive news of people we seldom see. We may also have flashes of inspiration and creativity, which should be followed, as success is likely. We may start to feel restless for no good reason. This is a communication card. Should the card be reversed, we may be concerned about a child in our environment, and news of others may be disturbing. Travel plans and business ventures will be delayed. We may find ourselves unable to make decisions.

Ace of Wands

A new child in the family, new start, new job, new house, new friendship, new romance - all these things are suggested when the Ace of wands is present in a spread. A creative phase is starting, and we will have a lot of fun and happiness along the way, as long as we hold on to our enthusiasm. Money worries are unlikely, or will lessen. Should the card be reversed, any new relationship may not be the passionate affair I q we had hoped it would be, and the whole thing may soon be a thing of the past. Plans may be cancelled or put back indefinitely and we will feel tense and disappointed. We should avoid rash decisions or chasing rainbows.

Two of Wands

A new project, new business, new aim in life are all suggested by this card. There could be opportunities for partnerships or joint ventures, which could mean moving away from present situations and places. Financial improvements are indicated, but we must have the courage to follow our intuition and take up opportunities offered. A forceful, successful man may be instrumental in furthering our aims. Promotions may be offered. Should the card be reversed, we are warned against unexpected loss and sorrow, and indeed anything unexpected. We should stand true to our hopes, and not let others who do not share our foresight restrict us in any way. Anxiety, frustration and uncertainty will feature in our lives; we may experience problems in relationships, either business or personal, and there will be delays.

Three of Wands

A good card for business, as it suggests enterprise and contractual progress through astute business sense and fortunate connections. Any partnerships will prove sound and worries are likely to be lessened. Travel connected with career is also suggested, and everything looks more than promising, leading to a feeling of happiness and optimism. Events may not yet have reached their true potential, but the signs are there that everything will turn out well, and all that is aimed for can be realised. Should the card be reversed, we should look for ulterior motives when people offer help or advice and beware of treachery. Try not to be too stubborn to see faults in projects or in other people. Be aware of opportunities, and although now may not be the time to actually go ahead with new projects, the situation will shortly improve and you should be ready to move when it does.

Four of Wands

A good card for romance and compatibility on a personal level. A feeling of peace and contentment comes with this card, both on a personal and business level. Any gatherings will be happy and convivial and monetary success is suggested. A feeling that it is now possible to indulge ourselves and contemplate purchase of property also likely. Should the card be reversed, we may feel uneasy and insecure. Romance looks unhappy and we feel that something is missing from our lives. Plans will be subject to delay and we are warned against taking anything for granted. Any property purchase may be severely delayed and may even have to be abandoned.

Five of Wands

This is a card indicating trial, struggle and difficulties. There are suggestions of conflict, arguments and dissatisfaction. If we are prepared to go all out for our aims and compete with and challenge others, we will succeed in the end, but not without a struggle. Negotiations and future expansions may be contemplated and legal matters are suggested. Nothing will run smoothly and there will be delays all round. We should pay attention to details and read all the small print before signing anything. We should also guard against apathy. Should the card be reversed, watch out for tricks and indecisiveness. People may misunderstand our motives, or we theirs, and court cases or legal action will prevent gains being made. Worry is likely. We should not give up but vow to try again.

Six of Wands

We reach a settlement of problems, and gains and victory are ours. All that is achieved has come about due to past efforts and this is our reward. We will find ourselves with more money than usual and feel happy with our lot. Any legal matters will be resolved favourably and progress is swift. We may find ourselves openly congratulated by others for our work or receive public acknowledgement. Promotions are also suggested. Should the card be reversed, delays again dog our path, and we may find ourselves wondering about those around us. Any benefits we have gained have been short-lived, and other people will seemingly always have the upper hand, and be likely to let us down badly when we rely on their help and advice. Anything connected with creative work is not well aspected.

Seven of Wands

This card suggests a victory despite other indications to the contrary. We must take advantage of situations, and as a result of hard effort, and despite possible competition from others, we will see the fruits of our labours. Anything creative looks favourable. We may have temporary health worries but these will pass. Should the card be reversed, we may find ourselves in embarrassing situations and doubtful of the way forward. We should try to be more decisive. Any problems should be resolved. However, we should be careful not to take on too much, as we may not be able to cope.

Eight of Wands

Things will start to move quickly and we will have boundless energy and enthusiasm. Advancement is suggested, and anxieties will reduce. We should watch, however, that we are not too hasty in business or personal dealings, as we will regret this. Travel or news from overseas is likely and romance looks promising. Should the card be reversed, arguments, rivalries and jealousies are possible and personal and domestic situations look fraught. Delays are apparent, plans will be cancelled. This is not a time to move forward.

Nine of Wands

Beware of things happening behind your back; expect the unexpected. Difficulties are likely and delays inevitable. Our inner strength will be called upon to see us through at this time. We should use this period of delay productively to plan for the future, rather than remaining stagnant and allowing frustrations to beset us. We should watch for opportunities and be certain of our facts before acting. Should the card be reversed, legal matters are suggested and things do not appear to be going according to plan. We may be feeling unwell and should take care of our health. We may suffer setbacks in our career, which will take their toll on our feeling of well-being. There are still more obstacles to deal with.

Ten of Wands

Responsibilities, tensions and pressures seem overwhelming, and we feel we are running hard yet getting nowhere. Perhaps we are being over ambitious, or maybe we are just being selfish in our aims. We should consider lessening our load and giving up certain plans, for the time being at least. We may find ourselves wanting to be involved in helping others at this time. Should the card be reversed, someone in our midst is trying to deceive us, and we must be careful. Losses are inevitable but, if we tread carefully, they can be minimised. We may feel trapped in a work situation, and colleagues will be less than helpful. However, a chance to move forward will eventually present itself. A romance may come to an abrupt end.

Practice

This chapter's questions concern the suit of wands.

- What colour hair and physical characteristics might you associate with the King of wands?
- We are about to go into business, and the Queen of wands appears as a prominent part of our reading. What does this indicate as far as the business venture is concerned?
- Give the other names by which the suit of wands may be known.
- What does the appearance of wands mean in general terms.
- What card amongst the suit of wands indicates a new child in the family?
- Along with the Queen of wands, we draw the three of wands.

The whole reading is concerning our prospective business venture. What does the three of wands tell us about this?

CHAPTER 5 – The Suit of Cups

Brief General Meanings

Cups, sometimes called chalices, goblets or coupes, as we have already established, represent the hearts in standard playing cards. They also have an affinity with religious groups or institutions. The people represented by the suit of cups are generally fair, plump people who are emotional, artistic, humane and creative. They are said to correspond to the water signs in the zodiac. Cups are associated with anything emotional, from marriage to personal possessions and concerns, which also covers anything relating to partnerships, whether in a work or personal context. Our relationships with others are covered by the suit of cups. It is a suit of love and happiness, and the feelings suggested by the suit run deep.

The Meanings of the Cards

King of Cups

The King of cups is a kind-hearted man, fair and plump, responsible and wise. Probably a professional person of some sort, he may have an interest in art or the arts, be a religious person, healer, counsellor or teacher. He is generous, both with his time and with his emotions, and is good with people of all ages. The presence of this card would indicate someone with these qualities will be able to help us in some way or that we ourselves should aim for these sorts of qualities. This person is reliable and well-meaning. We should listen to his advice, as we are likely to achieve a favourable outcome to anything we undertake as a result. Should the card be reversed, we should watch for legal difficulties, scandal or libel. Business contracts may be unwise or unfruitful, and those around us are not what they seem. The card could also indicate a person who is volatile, jealous and totally unreliable. We risk losing materially, professionally and personally should we follow the advice given by the person represented by the reversed King of cups.

Queen of Cups

The Queen of cups is a trusted lady, probably a beloved wife and/or mother, someone who has the benefit of experience through the years. She is honest, faithful and wise, with the benefit of foresight to help her through. The presence of the card can indicate a stable marriage and domestic happiness, or that good, sensible advice will come from a lady with these qualities. The card can also suggest a need for us to look into things more deeply and to develop an inner vision. Should the card be reversed, an emotional sacrifice may be necessary, or deception may occur in personal relationships. We are warned not to dismiss advice given. The card could represent a feeling of needing to be loved and wanted, which is missing in our lives, together with a feeling of inconsistency on the part of others. We should guard against anything immoral or dishonest.

Knight of Cups

An idealist, always on the look-out for opportunities, challenges or advancement. This card suggests that an invitation, job opportunity or proposal of some description is likely. As the card is one of arrival, something new may arrive on the scene, including new friends or people with whom we have lost touch. We will probably be feeling creative, optimistic and buoyant. Changes are on the horizon, and these could include romantic changes, or changes in emotions. We may fall in love with someone, or with an ideal. Travel is also suggested by this card. Should the card be reversed, we should beware of over-indulgences of any kind. Someone may be spreading gossip about us, and we should watch our behaviour, to avoid adding fuel to any speculations. We should also be careful in monetary dealings, and gambling is not well aspected, especially anything involving partnerships, as our choice of partner is suspect. Romance could be under a dark cloud.

Page of Cups

This card represents a thinker, someone who is naturally sensitive, reflective and altruistic, willing to help us in any way possible. The arrival of someone of this nature is suggested by the card. Anything connected with youngsters is well respected, and we may face new challenges or changes. This is a card of new birth, whether of a child or a project. This card could also herald a time of study or learning. Matters of a business nature will not proceed at great speed should this card appear in a spread. Should the card be reversed, we must beware of falling for the charms of someone who is shallow. Discretion is called for. We may miss opportunities and things will not turn out as expected. Problems with children may be expected. Any periods of study require extra concentration.

Ace of Cups

This is the true card of love, and all the emotions and traumas associated with love, being in love or falling in love. It is a happy card, bringing about a sense of fulfilment and peace. It is also a card which suggests psychic development or potential in some way, as well as the development of intuition. Anything undertaken will be productive and favourable, and happiness will be all around us in whatever we tackle. The birth of a child, an engagement or marriage are all suggested by this card. Things look promising for a new relationship.

Should the card be reversed, unwelcome changes are likely, and the feelings we have for someone are unlikely to be returned. This is the card of false friends and lovers, of inconsistency and unhappiness. We may find ourselves falling into a depression or despondency, thinking that events are not turning out as we had hoped.

Two of Cups

A good partnership or bond is suggested by the presence of this card. It is the card of harmony and unity. This could encompass both personal and business matters. The card suggests that matters can be healed, and peace restored after a situation of disharmony, or a partnership or marital split. Any problems with others in a working or business context should also begin to fade. This is a good card for those thinking of taking a partner. Should the card be reversed, there will be delays and opposition to any plans put forward. Quarrels with others may produce a parting of some sort, which may only be temporary but create problems. In a romantic sense, again a parting is suggested, probably due to infidelities, misunderstandings or conflicting aims and desires. We should guard against people who appear to be excessively charming, as they are not what they seem.

Three of Cups

A difficult situation is about to end and problems will be resolved. This is the healing card, and healing will surround us, physically, emotionally and spiritually. If we have been ill recently, we should now be feeling better. Things will turn out well in the end and we must have faith that this will be so. We may meet someone to whom we feel attracted or drawn, and this is the start of something good. Weddings, family gatherings and parties are likely.
A happy social life is suggested by this card. Our emotions are deep at this time. Should the card be reversed, we should watch our eating and drinking patterns, as problems are likely in this area. We will suffer from delays, and feel generally out of sorts. A partnership or friendship is likely to end, and we may find ourselves the target of someone's unwelcome attentions. Whilst we will still have a certain amount of fun, we are unlikely to find our soul-mate at this time.

Four of Cups

Now is the time to start making long-term plans. This is the card of new starts, new directions and new hope. Things will turn out a lot better than expected, and we should learn from this that optimism sometimes pays dividends. Whilst making plans, we should not expect to see much progress. This period has been allotted to us as a time when we can think things through without jeopardising other projects. We may feel under par or uneasy at this time. We need to recharge our batteries. We should watch our stress levels. Relationships, both personal and professional, may not be very satisfactory at this time and we may be feeling left out, unloved or unwanted. Resentment may rear its head, and we should try to avoid any confrontations. We may want to try a new relationship. Should the card be reversed, possibilities abound, and we are likely, having thought things through, to find an easy solution to something which has been bothering us for a long time. This is a good time to learn new things, join new social groups and meet new people.

Five of Cups

We are now finding it easier to deal with our lot in life. Any quarrels or splits are behind us, and we are starting to feel we can move on and away from the past. We are likely to find ourselves in the company of old and good friends, and may regret having lost touch in the past. Things may have gone wrong, but feeling sorry for ourselves is not the way out. Relationships may be difficult, and we may feel unloved, but we have something which we can work on for the future in other directions. We may find ourselves with extra money, through a small win or inheritance. Someone we meet now could have an effect on our lives in the long-term. Should the card be reversed, reunions are likely and rifts will be healed. The sense of loss remains, but things are not quite so bleak. True and trusted friends will rally round us and the outlook will seem more hopeful.

Six of Cups

We may feel nostalgic, thinking about our childhood and people who are no longer a part of our lives, and long to be able to turn back the clock, but we should realise that we are stronger from our experiences. The past is behind us, and we should now see that we can move forward with fresh hope. We should start to see progress in our endeavours, and our relationships become more stable. We are likely to find a use for skills we have put aside and creative talents will reappear. We are likely to find ourselves surrounded by family and friends. Should the card be reversed, whilst delays may occur and family concerns especially may not seem to be going according to plan, this is a good time for new opportunities, and we should keep our eyes open for their arrival. We should guard against being over suspicious or lethargic.

Seven of Cups

Sometimes we find ourselves daydreaming, and fantasy seems to be the easier option. Now is one of those times. However, we should guard against being unrealistic, foolish and unwise. We may be spoilt for choice in some situations. Daydreams have their place but we must realise that we are living in the real world. There is a lot of potential in emotional and financial situations, and we must deal with these realistically. This daydreaming phase can be turned to creativity with a bit of extra thought. We may be looking for some philosophical, religious or spiritual help or advice, and could be doing extra reading in this area. We may look full of confidence, but this is a front. Should the card be reversed, with strong-will and determination we are sure to win through in any situation. We will be logical and clear-thinking and will find solutions easily. Any confusion will be firmly in the past.

Eight of Cups

We are moving out of the darkness and into the light. Domestic and personal changes will take place. These will be beneficial, even though we may still find ourselves with upheavals to face, especially in personal or romantic issues. We could feel depressed, because we cannot face the idea of having to make further personal sacrifices. We may even find ourselves thinking of moving or in a new setting. Money, health and career prospects are well respected by this card. A modest or shy lady may prove helpful to us. We now know which plans to shelve and which to act on, and will do so, although we may not be prepared to put one hundred per cent effort into projects. Should the card be reversed, we are promised a lot of happiness in the future and family gatherings are likely.

Nine of Cups

A money card, signifying prosperity, abundance and success. This is also the card of good health and victory despite opposition. Any business deal or project is likely to be favourably respected, and we seem finally to be getting near personal goals. Emotionally we feel secure and content. A marriage is likely, possibly to someone older. We feel pleased with ourselves. Should the card be reversed, we will find difficulties and opposition continuing, and may suffer loss, due to mistakes or misplaced loyalties. Things may not turn out as hoped, and we are likely to make the wrong choices in business and/or personal matters. We should, however, not give up, but should try another avenue, as things may eventually go our way.

Ten of Cups

The card of the home and family. This card is love, happiness, peace, contentment and emotional harmony. Friendships, partnerships, relationships, marriages etc are all well respected by this card. Personal success is assured. This card is the summation of everything we could wish for, and more. There is a feeling of security and permanence. A birth in the family is possible. Should the card be reversed, quarrels and petty jealousies are likely. There will be problems within the family unit, and friendships will be strained.

There are likely to be continued problems at home and at work, but these will be short-lived. However, it is possible that a permanent split will occur. A feeling of sadness is likely, and a loss of status suggested. This card may indicate a divorce or personal separation, but before making any firm decisions on this, look to the other cards with which you are dealing, as the split may only be a temporary state of affairs.

Practice

This chapter's set of questions concerns the suit of cups.

- Give the other names by which the suit of cups may be known.
- How many cards are there in the suit of cups?
- What factors are covered by cups in general terms?
- A person refers to himself as the *Page of cups*. What qualities does he claim to possess?
- Someone is going through a bad patch in their marriage, and during their reading draws the two of cups. What does this suggest?
- The six of cups reversed comes into the reading. What does this mean?

CHAPTER 6 – The Suit of Pentacles

Brief, General Meanings

Pentacles are also called coins, money, circles, discs or deniers. They correspond to the suit of diamonds in the standard playing card pack, and, generally speaking, represent business or trades people, and business situations. As such, they are also the suit of possessions and financial matters. In general terms, pentacles as people are short and dark (or grey) and correspond to earth signs (Capricorn, Virgo, Taurus), displaying stubborn tendencies, a desire for status and a materialistic outlook. Pentacle people are practical and sensible, traditional and not normally interested in gambles.

The Meanings of the Cards

King of Pentacles

This is a person who is both reliable and trustworthy, not a gambler but a traditionalist. He is a sensible and mature business person, most probably grey haired, and frugal with money, as he needs to feel secure and safe. He offers sound financial advice and business contacts, and often represents someone in a position of authority, or with a legal connection. Should this card be present in a spread, we can expect to find ourselves with someone with these qualities, someone who is good with money and can advise us wisely and well. But this card is perhaps also suggesting we adopt these qualities ourselves. We are likely to find ourselves signing contracts, documents or papers, and business situations look promising. Should the card be reversed, we may still meet someone who seems to be a good business person, but in reality is not as successful as he would at first appear. We are warned to watch any involvement with such a man, as he may not be trustworthy. He may be spiteful, mean and vicious, and we are warned that we may be used by this person for his own ends. Family matters could be disruptive when this card appears in the reversed position within a spread. We should not enter into any legal contracts or sign documents at this time.

Queen of Pentacles

This is a generous lady whose sole interest seems to lie in making our life easier and offering chances of more money. She is sincere and trustworthy, practical and kind. She is a good communicator and generally gets what she wants from situations and from people. She is very skilled in domestic matters and is as happy in the home environment as she is in a career. The appearance of this card in a spread suggests an increase in money, status and possessions, and a move into a comfortable phase of existence. We could find ourselves meeting a rich, generous lady who could offer us money or help us find a way to earn more money in the future. She is a very good contact to have, and has a sensuality and self-sufficiency which are hard to ignore. Again, maybe the card is suggesting the emergence of these qualities within ourselves. Should the card be reversed, any increase in earnings or possessions will be short-lived, and we may find ourselves in the company of a lady who is not to be trusted, and end up losing in some way because of her. It is also possible that this lady may just be going through a spell of misfortune and will bounce back in time, and that this situation could be a mirror image of events in our own life. We are told to rely on ourselves rather than others when this card appears in a spread and whilst we may find our enthusiasm at a low ebb, we must be prepared to work hard to get out of the rut we are in.

Knight of Pentacles

KNIGHT of PENTACLES

This man has the appearance of immaturity, and while he is responsible, trustworthy, methodical and hard-working, he has not yet developed the strength of character needed to win through in business situations. He is a good executive, but not yet capable of moving up the corporate ladder. He is likely to offer suggestions and ideas which we should consider, even though he may not have thought them through properly. However, we should not be too willing to take him on as part of a package. The presence of this card in a spread suggests a need to learn, to be innovative and to see things through to their logical conclusion. In certain circumstances this card can relate to someone who is out of work, but who has a lot of ideas and needs some backing. This card can also indicate travel associated with work. Should the card be reversed, we are warned to watch out for someone who is trying to trip us up in a business sense. This is also the card of not thinking things through and lack of foresight. We should guard against a lack of direction, limited vision and apathy, which would lead to stagnation and feelings of frustration. It is possible that this card could herald problems in a business sense, and that it is necessary to draw in the purse strings a little.

Page of pentacles

A card of study, research and desire for knowledge. We may be embarking on a period of learning to enhance our career prospects, or alternatively we may be meeting someone whose love of learning and quest for new ideas will help us on our way. Often this card can indicate someone whom we meet by chance, and brings about the possibility of advancement, promotion or success. The Page in all situations is generally someone who is relatively young, and this card is promising for youngsters within a family situation, especially for those who are interested in studying commerce or business management. It is also a good card for anyone in the fitness professions, as it is a healthy and happy card. Good news is suggested by this card, possibly extra money by way of a windfall or legacy. A hobby or interest could turn into something profitable.

Should the card be reversed, there could be money difficulties and problems with young people in the home, who may become rebellious and demanding. The card also warns of the necessity to face facts and dismiss ideas which are merely flights of fancy and which have no logic. Should we ignore the warnings, losses could result. We should also watch for someone who is totally unreliable.

Ace of Pentacles

A good money card, especially for people who gamble, speculate or take risks with money. Success is certain and riches will come, either from our own personal efforts or through a win or legacy. It can also be seen to be the card of spiritual as well as material riches, and we may find ourselves in the company of someone whose effect upon our lives will be profound. This person could be either a spiritual mentor or someone in a business sense, but the partnership has splendid possibilities. When this card appears in a spread, we can expect promotions, wage increases or a chance to move to a more highly paid and more prestigious job. We will be blessed with an abundance of energy and the drive and determination to work for our goals. Should the card be reversed, delays may be around us, and we may also waste chances or money. Gambles may still be profitable, but we will not feel happy with the resultant success, but become greedy, mean and avaricious.

Two of Pentacles

Circumstances will improve slowly, and we will have to be very clever in using our funds to their best advantage. Working and social situations are likely to be happy, yet new projects will seem to be slow starters and we will be anxious about the outcome. Life will not be easy for a time. We must, however, be prepared to take risks and act when opportunities are presented. It is also possible that there is a situation where money will have to be paid out to a partner or friend. Troubles seem around every corner. Should the card be reversed, communications from others will lead to new prospects of advancement and we will feel a little more buoyant. It is possible that we will find ourselves working flat out and getting nowhere, and we may find ourselves dealing with paperwork more, both for business and pleasure. When in the reverse position, this is a good card for those embarking on a literary career, although some decisions may not go in our favour for a while.

Three of Pentacles

Success through hard work and effort is suggested by this card. It is the card of the tradesman, artist or builder, and augurs well for those people who are wishing to undertake any DIY scheme or major renovation project on property. The card also indicates success in exams, projects, business and personal matters. It is a card suggesting the profitability of a new enterprise, whether artistic, literary or personal. Hard work will be necessary, but the result looks more than promising. This is the card of good starts. Should the card be reversed, we are likely to find ourselves short of funds, lacking in ideas and motivation, and with difficulties in our relationships. Indifference should be guarded against. We are unlikely to find others very cooperative, and our ultimate career aims seem to be overshadowed by lethargy.

Four of pentacles

This is the card of King Midas, the hoarder of money, lover of wealth and luxury, the miserly person. Money is not everything, and while we need financial and material security, there are other matters of equal or greater importance which must be addressed at this time. We may find ourselves in receipt of extra money and feel like putting it away for a rainy day. We may also think of investments at this time. We must however, be sure to be a little generous to those around us, and to ourselves. We may fear loss, but there is nothing to fear save fear itself. Should the card be reversed, we may find our pay cheque delayed, or some money due slow getting to us. Things will not be going according to plan at all, and we will find ourselves held back in some way; obstacles will be forever in our path. We should also watch our spending when the card is reversed, as there is a tendency to be rash, or spend money we do not have.

Five of pentacles

A good card for romance and affairs of the heart, but not necessarily so for money matters. We may feel the need to make plans for the future, but mistakes are more than likely and now is not the time to take risks, as failure is suggested. Family and friends are likely to be helpful to us at this time and offer emotional support, which is badly needed, as we are feeling a sense of loss of faith in our abilities. We must try to rise to the challenge, and draw on our inner strength. We cannot live in the past; we must be realistic. Should the card be reversed, relationships may cause problems, but things will be turning in our favour and business interests become more promising. This is the card for someone who is emerging from a business loss, bankruptcy or setback, as it suggests things are finally turning round. A solution to problems will be found.

Six of Pentacles

The generosity of others will rub off on us, and we may feel more inclined to offer monetary support to others. This could, of course, also indicate that money will have to be shared because of a divorce or separation. It is the card of charity work, altruism and kindness. Through giving, we will receive. Any purchases made now are likely to be good and sound, and business transactions or expansions will be favourable. We may meet someone who offers financial support to a new venture. Our faith in human nature and in ourselves will be restored. Should the card be reversed, we may find ourselves with bad debts, loans we cannot pay, or conversely, a period when loans are coming to an end. This is the card, when reversed, of financial commitments and obligations. It is also a card suggesting a period of financial insecurity. We should guard against envy of others and selfish attitudes. Ultimately, we will be the loser, if these emotions are allowed to take hold.

Seven of Pentacles

Progress, albeit slow, is assured. Another card suggesting gain and improvement in circumstances, through hard work and effort. We may find ourselves receiving encouraging news and any opportunities to combine business with pleasure should be grasped. Others will be more than helpful to us at this time. We will feel quite satisfied, although we may feel we could do with a little more action. There are some decisions to make but we must think things through before taking action. This is the card of steady progress rather than a quick rise to the top. Should the card be reversed, delays are likely, complications will beset us and speculations will not turn out to be viable. We will feel anxious and uneasy. Unwise actions are now reeking their revenge. We may feel like giving up altogether, but should hang on and bide our time until trends improve. We should watch others at this time, as the card suggests gossip and people who are untrustworthy.

Eight of pentacles

A new job, chances to develop new skills and talents are suggested by this card. It is a card of development of potential. It is possible that a hobby or creative talent can be turned into a profitable business, and we will find ourselves rapidly picking up new talents and skills which, if utilised correctly, will help our career advancement. Again it is a card suggesting effort and hard work, and often a period of apprenticeship. We may find ourselves the recipients of a small windfall, and friendships will be good. We may also find ourselves wishing to help or train others with skills we have already developed. Should the card be reversed, we are likely to experience a loss of some sort, and problems in our careers will overshadow us. We should not lend money, offer help which we cannot deliver, or undertake any loans at this time. We may find ourselves in the company of people who are charming yet insincere.

We will feel disillusioned and unhappy.

Nine of Pentacles

Things are going well and according to plan. We feel contented with our lot, happy, safe and secure. We have worked hard, and now we can reap the benefits of our work. Money and success are around the corner. Everything looks good for us, both at home and at work. Negotiations undertaken at this time are likely to be profitable long-term and expansion prospects are good. This is a card suggesting that we may now start to look outside our immediate environment at other cultures and settings. It may also suggest a period when our intuition is sound. Should the card be reversed, gambles will not payoff, we may lose a friend or possession and delays and frustrations will be apparent. It is possible that job losses will occur, or projects will not come to fruition. We may not have used our money wisely or made provision for difficult times. We are warned to look for double-dealings and people who have ill-intent. Despite a possible lack of funds, we may feel the need to make purchases, especially household items or even new furniture.

Ten of Pentacles

A period of contentment, security and wealth is suggested by this card. It is a family card, and therefore suggests inheritances or legacies, as well as family comforts and the happiness of family gatherings. Sometimes this card can be seen as suggesting the need to make provisions for others within the family, either by making a will, deed of gift, taking out a pension, or by undertaking a

project which will ultimately make the family unit more secure. Should we be thinking of moving house or enlarging the house we already have, this card suggests we should act. Travel and movement are well aspected. Should the card be reversed, we may find ourselves restricted in some way. Success will come, but not yet. Our reputation in business may be on the line and we are warned against bad risks, gambling, robbery and loss. We will not be feeling emotionally or personally secure when this card appears in the reversed position. We should take steps to secure our possessions. A feeling of being ill-at-ease will pervade and a lack of money or loss of financial security will intensify the sensation. However,
restrictions will ease after a time; we need to learn to develop
patience and serenity during these times of difficulty.

Practice

This chapter's questions concentrate on the suit of pentacles.

• What other names may the suit of pentacles be called?
• The King of pentacles reversed comes up in the reading for a person who is just about to sign a contract to buy some land. What does the card suggest?
• We are just about to take a risk on the Stock Exchange, and draw the Ace of pentacles. What does this suggest?
• Following on from the previous question, we also draw the nine of pentacles. Does this fit in with the other card, and what does it add to the information we already have?

CHAPTER 7 – Spreads

Having looked at both the major and minor arcana, we will now discuss a few sample spreads. If you feel a little unsure about some of the cards, don't worry. It can take time before all the various meanings of the cards have registered sufficiently to allow you to interpret cards without a prompt every now and again. There are many types of spread, and the following are but a few. You may find your own spread and feel happy with that, rather than following any of these.

Hints on Giving a Reading

If you undertake a reading for a friend, you take on a big responsibility - do not abuse it! Never present information as the absolute truth or suggest that there is no room for choice. The cards produce one way of looking at problems; they do not give all the answers.

Certain messages are given in the cards, and it is important that these are emphasised. The questions and concerns of the person for whom the reading is being done must also be taken into account. The main emphasis should always be on a positive ultimate outcome. It is important that anyone consulting the cards is given direct advice which will help them, and that their attention is focused on the problems in a positive way. Even if the cards indicate continuing problems, show that these things are necessary at this time, and that by discovering and understanding the true nature of the problems, a solution will eventually be presented. Should all the cards be negative, try to concentrate on the fact that these things are being shown together for a purpose, and try to discover this purpose.

The Ten Card Spread

As you will see from the illustration above, this spread covers past, present and future. Using this spread as an example, try shuffling your own cards and see what cards you get. Remember to read each card individually, and then look at the picture as a whole.

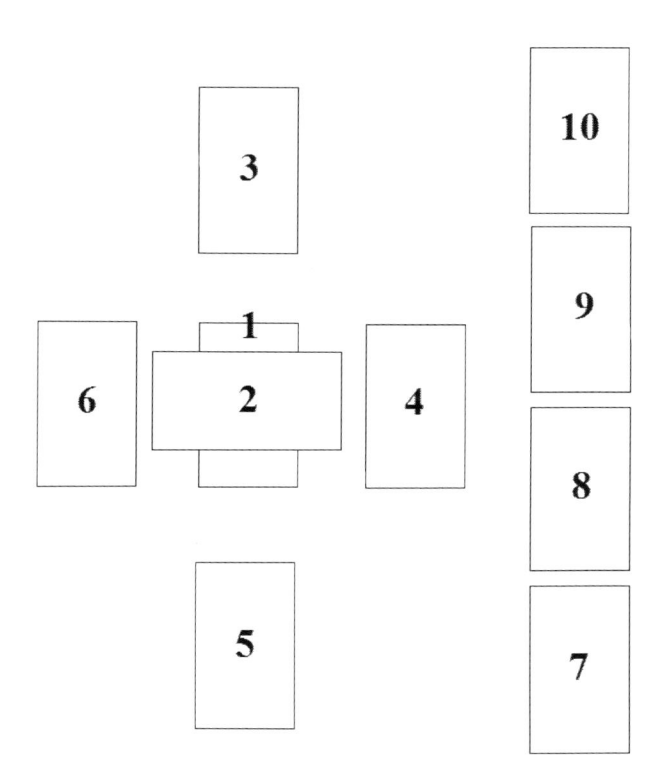

Key
CARD 1 = Present
CARD 2 = Immediate obstacles
CARD 3 = Specific goal
CARD 4 = Past foundations
CARD 5 = Past
CARD 6 = Future
CARD 7 = The questioner
CARD 8 = Environmental factors
CARD 9 - Inner emotions
CARD 10 = Final result

The Seven Card Spread

Another spread you can try is the seven card spread, shown below. Again, you will see that we have cards for the past, present and future.

[1][2][3][4][5][6][7]

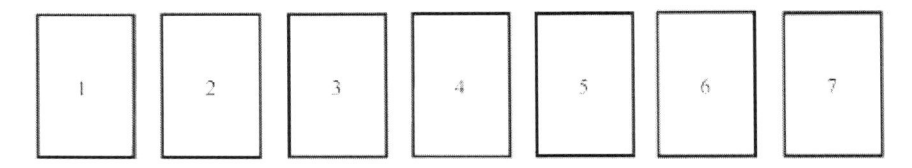

Key

CARD 1 = Distant Past
CARD 2 = Immediate past
CARD 3 = Present Influences
CARD 4 = Present Obstacles
CARD 5 = Present Outlook
CARD 6 = Future influences
CARD 7 = End Results

The Bohemian Spread

One of the popular spreads used by professional tarot readers is the Bohemian spread. This spread deals with some of the major points most people need to address, and any seven cards can be chosen from the shuffled pack.

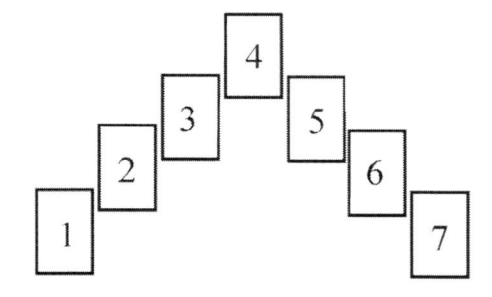

Key

CARD 1 = Home and domestic matters
CARD 2 = Wishes, fears and desires
CARD 3 = Relationships, friendships and love
CARD 4 = Hoped for achievements
CARD 5 = Obstacles and unexpected assistance
CARD 6 = Immediate future and possibilities
CARD 7 = Good fortune

As you can see from the above breakdown, most people have an interest in at least four of the categories and so for this reason many professional tarot readers will use this method. It is quick and easy to remember, and above all, it is effective.

The Pyramid

In recent years, there has been an increased interest in anything Egyptian, and as a result it is no surprise to see a spread called the pyramid.

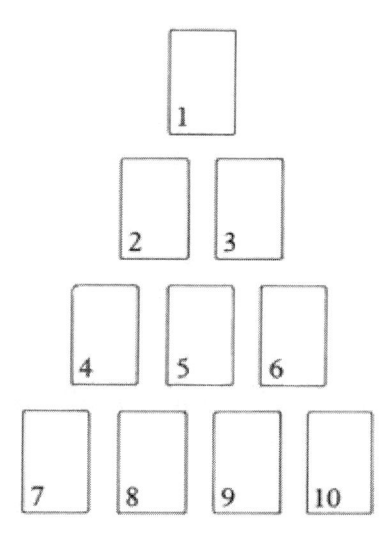

```
         1
      2     3
    4    5    6
  7    8    9    10
```

Key

CARD 1 = Main circumstances prevailing
CARD 2 = Alternatives worth considering
CARD 3 = Alternatives worth considering
CARD 4, 5 and 6 = Events which led to present circumstances and the forces at work behind the scenes
CARD 7, 8, 9, and 10 = Best way in which we can either resolve the problems or deal with them

This is another easy spread to use, and is particularly successful in helping with specific problems or difficulties which may be present. Having shuffled the pack, any 10 cards can be used and are dealt in the order as shown above.

The 12-Month Spread

You may find it useful to learn the 12-month spread. As may be obvious from its name, this spread concentrates on each month of the year and so can be particularly useful for those people who want to know when something may happen or know about something relating to a particular month.

The cards can be laid in any way, but probably two rows of six cards is the most logical.

There are several ways of looking at this spread, but the most usual way is to take the present month as Month 1, and work through until you reach Month 12. Sometimes this spread may also be called the calendar spread because it is based on months. Remember to look at each individual card as well as the whole picture, and to work out the relationship to the previous card to see how the year will progress. You may wish to use the minor arcana only for this particular spread, although I have seen people using the full tarot pack.

Whilst considering the months of the year, it may be worth noting that it is said that each suit of the minor arcana is linked to a season of the year. Pentacles are said to relate to the winter months of December, January and February. Swords relate to the spring months of March, April and May, wands relate to the summer months of June, July and August and cups relate to the autumn months of September, October and November. Taking all this into account, it is possible to learn whether a problem will be resolved, and approximately during which month.

To do this, merely take the cards, both major and minor arcarna, and then shuffle them well. Divide them into three packs, and taking one pack, deal out 12 cards. If a month card (or cards) appears within the 12, it is possible that matters will be resolved during that month or months. If no month card appears, it is possible that the problem will remain unresolved for the next 12 months.

The 21-Card Spread

Another spread which can be used is the 21-card spread. This again can help with future developments, but requires skill and a great deal of practice to use properly, bearing in mind the number of cards used and the categories into which these fall. It is probably a spread to aim for when you have practised the others several times first.

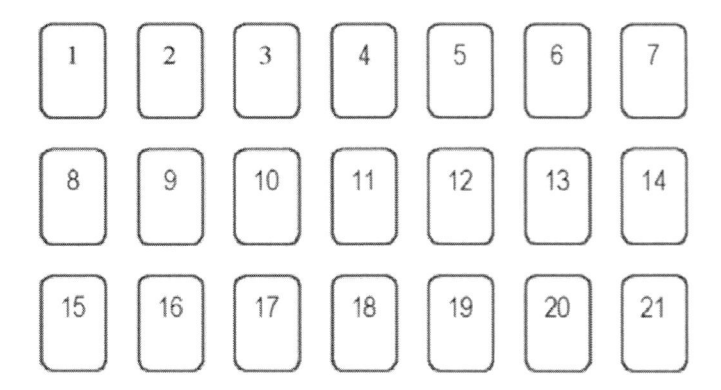

Key

Column 1 = The person concerned and their present state (1, 8 and 15)
Column 2 = The situation around the person (2, 9 and 16)
Column 3 = The hopes and fears of the person (3, 10 and 17)
Column 4 = Expectations (4, 11, and 18)
Column 5 = The unexpected (5, 12, and 19)
Column 6 = The near future (6, 13 and 20)

Column 7 = The long-term future. (7, 14 and 21)

Many people use this spread when dealing with problems of career and home, although obviously it can be used for any area of difficulty. It is always worth bearing in mind what we have learnt about month cards in this spread, and indeed others, as it might then be possible to be more specific on the timing of events, especially when dealing with things to come.

The Five Card Spread

The spread which I use most often is the five card spread. To obtain the five cards to be used, I ask the person to shuffle the cards and then take them back and ask for five numbers which have a meaning to the person concerned, count out these numbers from the top of the shuffled pack and lay the cards so obtained in the following pattern:

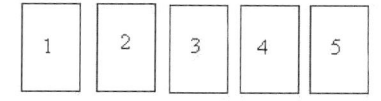

| 1 | 2 | 3 | 4 | 5 |

A Sample Reading

Using this spread, let's do a sample reading. As you will see from the illustration above, all the cards are numbered. They are laid out in this particular way to form two pages of a book, with the third card being the binding holding the two pages together or, alternatively, preventing the pages being turned over. They do not fall into a past, present and future theme, as such, and again it is important to read the whole story from the cards.

Card 1 - Hermit from major arcana
Card 2 - Page of cups from minor arcana
Card 3 - The Devil card from major arcana
Card 4 - Nine of swords from minor arcana
Card 5 - Six of wands from minor arcana

What sort of things would you say, should you do a reading for someone and these cards result? Let's pretend this reading is for a lady of 40, a career woman, who may want to start a new project. She is unmarried but has a relationship of long standing.

In very brief terms, there is a retreat of some sort going on, with the person concerned turning inwards and doing a lot of thinking. Decisions have to be made, and a patient attitude is needed. Perhaps things are not moving quickly enough for the lady, and she feels frustrated. The Page of cups would indicate that study may also be necessary (perhaps she has got to do more research into her new project) and that things will not move forward very quickly.

Maybe the person concerned will offer her services to someone. The Devil card indicates that there are certain commitments and ties and that there is a need for freedom from restraint. Again, a reassessment is necessary, and the person concerned should guard against being tied to something or someone against their will. This probably accounts for the feelings put forward in the Hermit and

Page of cups cards, as the Devil card, being the third card, is the card holding together the other four cards. The nine of swords is a worry card; there are worries involved as a result of the restrictions being placed upon the person. There are also probably family worries, unhappiness and quarrels. However, the six of wands card indicates that everything will turn out fine in the end, problems will be overcome and delays lifted.

This is a short resume, and not the way in which a reading would normally be done. I have only given the briefest of meanings on each card, so you can get the gist and then add on your own interpretations.

All the necessary information to carry out a tarot reading has been given, but it takes practice to perfect the art, and you must not set yourself unrealistic goals as to when you are going to be proficient enough to carry out readings without referring to this book from time to time.
I hope that this introduction to the tarot will lead you to further investigation and reading on the subject, and that you will ultimately enjoy interpreting the cards for yourself and others.

Practice

The final set of questions will review some of the things we have learnt in the course of this book. We have undertaken a reading for a close friend who draws the following cards:

Ace of pentacles
King of swords
Hermit
Justice reversed
Two of cups

• In general terms, do these cards suggest a favourable outcome, and how would the Hermit card as the third card in the spread of five relate? What special meaning, if any, should we attach to this card?
• Someone draws ten cards, of which eight are swords. What would this immediately suggest to you?
• Using a seven card spread, the second card drawn is the three of pentacles. What would this suggest, and what period of time would the card represent?

Conclusions

Many people, having learnt from using tarot that there is a definite link between the conscious mind and the psyche or subconscious mind, may be interested to see the relationship that tarot has with other forms of self-help.

Many psychologists acknowledge that the story of the major arcana has a definite relationship with our journey through life.

Transpersonal psychologists, for example, now sometimes use the story of the Fool to explain to clients the growth of the human soul from immaturity through to happiness and fulfilment; the story of the Fool's journey is as valuable in the twentieth century as it was in medieval times.
Mankind may be more advanced, and consider himself (or herself) more civilised, but the same problems beset us now in our modern age as beset our ancestors, albeit in different forms. If we can learn to tap into our inner wisdom and seek help from sources such as tarot, we can grow as human beings and become better people as a result.

Other Links

There is a definite link between tarot and astrology and, as we have seen, the cards of the minor arcana are connected to the elements of earth, air, fire and water in the same way as are the signs of the zodiac.

It is often possible to link the cards to particular zodiac signs when doing a reading and this applies not only to the minor arcana but also to the major. Many feel that the Justice card, for example, has obvious links with Libra, and its presence within a spread could always indicate the intervention or help of a Libran person in a situation. It is not just the sword cards in the minor arcana which may have Libran links! Strength, or La Force, is another card which can link with a zodiac sign, in this case that of Leo. Make sure you look at such connections or at least consider them when undertaking a reading.

If you are interested in finding out more about astrology, you may like to read Star Signs for Beginners, another book in this series.

In my work, tarot and numerology link very well, and again this is something you may wish to consider. Numerology for Beginners will give you information on the systems and the relevance of numbers in our daily lives, and you may like me, end up combining these two ancient forms.

Final Thoughts

Be sure that the help received from the tarot is acknowledged. Treat your cards with respect and with care, and they will provide years of help and enjoyment.

Printed in Great Britain
by Amazon